Prayer Is a Welcome Place

A USER-FRIENDLY GUIDE TO PRAYER

B E T S Y   L E E

*Reaching, refreshing, healing and
empowering through Christ.*

Bloomington, Minnesota

Cover and illustrations by Anne Baumgartner.

Layout by Susan Kes.

Library of Congress Catalog Card Number 99-93354

ISBN: 0-9673557-0-2

Dedication

To Maureen Magnuson,
partner and friend.

What a joy to be on the journey with you!

Acknowledgments

This book was written in community. The initial inspiration came while I was studying Henry Blackaby's *Experiencing God* with a group of eight women. When we began to meet, I saw a prayer picture of all eight of us climbing into a hot air balloon. We were in for a great adventure. . . up, up, up we went. Several years later we are still experiencing God in new ways, still flying high in the Spirit.

During the course of this study, I thought to myself, *Wouldn't it be fun to write a book to help people experience God through prayer in groups like this?* My friends—Mary Bertelson, Kathy Coleman, Pamela Jensen, Karen Jones, Maureen Magnuson, Linda Nyvall, and Teresa VanCleave—loved the idea. They not only prayed for me as I wrote this book, but they also test-marketed it in our group as it was being written. Many thanks to each of you.

God then put together a team of top-notch professionals to make the book attractive and inviting to read. I am grateful to Anne Baumgartner, Susan Kes, Terry McDowell, and Jim Iverson.

Finally, I'd like to thank the Colonial Church of Edina Foundation and the Getsch Family Foundation for their generous support of this project.

Contents

Introduction

Is prayer a delight or a duty for you? Something you dread or something you truly enjoy? Perhaps you sense that there is more to prayer than blessings at meals and bedtime. Perhaps you know there's more, but you aren't sure how to find out what that is.

The purpose of this book is to expand your vision of prayer: to suggest new and different ways to pray, to help you discover the joy of praying with others, and finally, to inspire you to reach out and touch the lives of others through your prayers.

This prayer guide can be read in two ways, either individually or read and discussed in a group. It is my hope that small groups will be able to use this resource in a variety of settings: adult education classes on Sunday morning, midweek fellowship groups, home Bible studies, or prayer groups.

There are six chapters, which makes it an ideal six-week study. At the end of each chapter, you will find a personal exercise to enrich your own prayer life and group discussion questions for those who are reading and discussing the book together. Space is provided after each question for you to write down thoughts for your own reflection and to share with the group. The discussion questions are followed by a prayer exercise to try as a group.

Whether you read this book on your own or with a group, I hope that you find it a lot of fun to read. Anne's whimsical line drawings, I'm sure, will make the text more inviting and friendly. A book about prayer—just like prayer itself—should be imaginative and creative, exciting and fresh.

As you read this book, may you feel increasingly at home and at ease in God's presence. Let prayer become a welcome place, relaxing, enjoyable, a place you love to be.

Betsy Lee
June 4, 1999

Chapter 1

A Welcome Place

Prayer is a place in our hearts where we meet God. A place where we can truly relax and be ourselves. A place where we are received with pleasure, hospitality, and glad acceptance. A welcome place.

Imagine coming home from a hard day, perhaps loaded down with groceries or extra work from the office. As you walk through the door exhausted, a loving Friend takes the load you are carrying. "Here," He says. "Let me help you with that." He takes these things and puts them aside, then invites you into the living room. "Now," He smiles, "tell me about your day." As your Friend listens with sympathy and understanding, you feel completely at ease and free to share your deepest feelings.

Sometimes you don't need to say anything at all. You just enjoy being with Him. He helps you see things from a different perspective. What were you so worried about? After being in the company of this understanding Friend, you feel lighter, freer, filled with new energy and resolve.

Jesus is that kind of Friend and prayer can be that comfortable and inviting. We all need such a friend, and we all need to create spaces in our lives where we can receive the rest, refreshment, and love that Jesus offers, and that we so desperately need.

Is prayer a welcome place for you? Do you feel at home and at ease in God's presence? The purpose of this book is to suggest practical, concrete ways that prayer can be friendlier, more accessible, and more enjoyable—a place where you can draw near to God so that He can draw near to you (James 4:8).

Prayer has not always been a welcome place for me. Enjoying prayer as much as I do now has been a learning process. I am still learning. The insights I share in these pages have come over many years of growing in prayer, gleaning a great deal of wisdom from other people, and gradually allowing the Holy Spirit to reveal to me just how deeply I am loved by God and how much He wants to be a part of my life.

My Prayer Journey

Prayer is based on a love relationship with God, and like any relationship, it has to develop. Prayer evolves from simple, childlike prayers at meals and bedtime to sharing personal problems with God as an adolescent to struggling with the challenges of faith as an adult, hard things that either turn us away from God or draw us closer.

The first definition I heard as a child of this mysterious process was "prayer is talking to God." My parents valued prayer, and they helped me learn to pray, but more than their methods, what I remember most is their understanding that God is loving and I could experience that love by knowing Jesus.

The more I came to know Jesus, the deeper my prayer life became and the more connected I felt to God. God was not just an abstract entity. He was personal and real.

However, I never guessed how real God could be until one day I asked my friend Nancy how she prayed. I was sitting on the edge of her bed at the time, a few feet from where she was sitting. "Well," she said, "when I pray, I picture Jesus sitting next to me, about as close as you are to me now, and I talk to Him just like I would talk to you."

This thought was revolutionary to me. Nancy was describing a personal, relaxed intimacy with God that I had never experienced. Yes, I talked to God. Yes, I felt His presence, but not like Nancy did. She was describing the difference between talking to a statue and a real person, between shouting into the universe and having a dialogue with Someone who cares.

Could you really picture God that close to you? Why not? One of the names for God in the Bible is *Jehovah-Shammah*, the "God who is present." In the Old Testament, God is depicted as a loving Father who carries the Israelites in His everlasting arms as they wander for forty years in the wilderness (Deuteronomy 33:27), a God who hears the cries of His people and responds with compassion (2 Kings 20:5), a God not made of stone but One who longs to be actively involved in their lives.

Still people thought of God as distant. So He sent His Son, Jesus—*Immanuel*, "God with us"—to walk among men and women to reveal Himself in ways they could understand. God is love and Jesus was love personified. Wherever He went, He demonstrated God's desire to touch people's lives very specifically and very personally.

Scripture says that "Jesus Christ is the same yesterday and today and forever" (Hebrews 13:8).

If Jesus revealed the invisible God in visible ways to people two thousand years ago, why wouldn't He be doing the same thing today? Why wouldn't He long to be as actively involved in *our* lives?

As soon as I became aware of this, I started to read the Bible with a new sense of immediacy and excitement. I imagined myself as one of Jesus' disciples, hearing His footsteps next to mine as we walked miles on long, dusty roads. I watched Him move among the crowds and look with compassion on the sick and hurting. He touched the blind and they could see, the crippled and they could walk. Once on a stormy sea, He spoke peace and brought an inexplicable calm.

I saw how deeply Jesus cared for people and began to realize how deeply He cared for me. I needed Him to calm the storms in my life, to heal my hurts, to help me see things that I could not see.

As I immersed myself in Scripture, I began to develop eyes of faith to see God at work all around me, to sense His presence—to even hear His voice.

Prayer for me became not just a time to talk to God, but also a time to listen. One day as I stood at my infant daughter's bedroom door, I watched her rouse from an afternoon nap. I thought of Jesus' words: "Your Father knows what you need before you ask him" (Matthew 6:8). I knew from experience that my daughter would soon rub the sleep from her eyes and cry from hunger. *How much more completely must God know us*, I thought. *And how much more attentive He is to our needs!*

This realization was only one of many that flooded my mind during those early years of parenting. As I cared for my daughter, God continued to reveal to me very specific things about how He loved me as His daughter. He also showed me how understanding His love as a Father could equip me to be a better parent. This led to my book *Miracle in the Making.*[1]

A strange thing happened to me when I became a mother. I became more open and vulnerable, more compassionate, so much so that when I entered a room of strangers, I began to hear the "heart cries" of adults, hidden cries they were often not aware of themselves.

As I developed a piercing sense of pain in people's lives, I drew closer to God's heart and actually felt what He felt. I began to share *His* grief when I saw men and women hurting, *His* longing to wipe away tears, *His* yearning to mend the broken pieces of their lives. My prayer life intensified and changed from not only talking and listening to God, but also partnering with Him.

I am not a people person. By nature, I am shy, reticent, a loner, but God changed all that. God *is* a people person. His heart goes out to people who are hurting. When a relationship is broken, when we suffer loss or disappointment, or feel rejected, He suffers too—and wants to respond. *Who will go to love and comfort and dry a tear?* He seemed to be asking. Much to my surprise, I said, "Here I am. Send me."

As I moved out into ministry, prayer was no longer a luxury, an optional part of my day. It became an absolute necessity. I felt inadequate, ill-equipped, and completely dependent on God. Prayer was the only way I could receive the guidance and instruction I needed to do what God asked me to do.

I was always struck in the Bible by the many times Jesus went off by Himself to pray—sometimes He spent all night praying. Why? Because that's where He got His guidance and instruction. Jesus said that He only did what the Father told Him to do. "The words I say to you are not just my own," He said. "Rather, it is the Father, living in me, who is doing his work" (John 14:10). If Jesus needed to pray to hear from God, how much more do we!

As I pressed on in prayer, I discovered that I needed to come to know the third Person of the Trinity, the Holy Spirit. It is the Holy Spirit who empowers us for ministry. Jesus told His disciples,

"You will receive power when the
Holy Spirit has come upon you"
(Acts 1:8). Just as Jesus was
dependent on God's Spirit
to empower His ministry,
the same gift would be
given to them—and
to us.

In John 14:16 the Holy Spirit is called the
Helper. He reveals God's truth to us (John 16:13);
He gives us specific guidance (Isaiah 30:21); He
gives us wisdom and understanding (Isaiah 11:2);
He gives us confidence (2 Timothy 1:7); He helps
us to do things that would be impossible on our
own (Acts 1:8).

Whether you are in ministry, raising a family, or
striving to be an ethical businessperson, living out a
life of love in an unloving world requires the help
of the Holy Spirit. His help comes through the
guidance, conviction, and inspiration of a vibrant
prayer life.

Your Prayer Journey

What about your prayer journey? Where has
your journey taken you? What new directions are
you eager to explore? As Jack Taylor says, prayer is
"life's limitless reach."[2] Despite all the books, classes, and seminars about prayer we have today, I

believe we still stand on the threshold of the frontiers of prayer. There is so much to learn.

Life's limitless reach? Right now your biggest challenge may be just squeezing out five minutes from a busy schedule to pray. I remember when my children were small, I once stole away in the downstairs bathroom and shut the door to pray. All around me were strewn a sea of shoes on the floor; I sat in the corner in a two-foot square empty spot. That's what my life felt like then—crowded, cluttered, with no time to think, much less pray! But that's when God taught me some of my most creative ways to pray.

Perhaps when you do set aside time to pray, you find your mind flitting every which-way, completely unable to concentrate. I have a friend like that. She said one day God showed her a picture of herself as a car pulling into a gas station, needing to be filled up, but darting here and there so that the attendant couldn't put the gas nozzle in the tank. God wanted to fill her with His love, but she needed to be still to receive it. She laughed and cried at the same time, realizing how ridiculous she looked, and yet saddened by her inability to let God love her. My friend later learned specific things she could do to calm her racing mind and be more open and receptive in prayer.

Guilt may be a struggle for you. Am I praying enough? Am I praying the right way? What happens if, heaven forbid, I fall asleep while praying? Dan, a pastor friend of mine, did that. His wife came downstairs one morning and found him at the dining room table, sound asleep, with his Bible open. He felt guilty that he had fallen asleep.

"Don't," said Kathy. "You've just fallen asleep in the lap of the Lord."

Dan's eyes lit up. "You're right. Why can't I just say, 'Daddy, I'm sleepy.'"

Prayer is a welcome place. A place where you should feel at ease. There is no right way or wrong way to do it. No specific time, no specific location. Find what works for you and know that God delights in spending time with you—even if you do fall asleep or you aren't able to set aside time with Him as often as you'd like.

This book is full of practical tips that should make your prayer life easier. At the end of each chapter, I've included a prayer exercise you can try and several discussion questions you can share if you are studying this book in a group.

It doesn't matter where you are on your prayer journey, but it is important to know that prayer is a journey. Prayer is a process, something we grow in day by day. Let's encourage one another, learn from each other, and spur each other on to try new things in prayer.

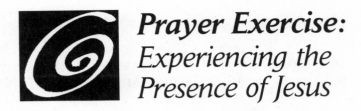

Prayer Exercise:
Experiencing the Presence of Jesus

I mentioned that I could sense the presence of Jesus in a more exciting and immediate way when I learned to imagine myself as a participant in a Scripture scene. Would you like to try this?

Open up all your senses, your imagination. Come as a child, open, trusting, ready to receive God's love. Read the following words of Scripture, then close your eyes. In silence or while listening to relaxing music, imagine yourself in this scene. Let the action unfold in your mind. Slowly, gradually, let it draw you in. . .

Then they brought little children to Him, that He might touch them; but the disciples rebuked those who brought them. But when Jesus saw it, He was greatly displeased and said to them, "Let the little children come to Me, and do not forbid them; for of such is the kingdom of God. Assuredly, I say to you, whoever does not receive the kingdom of God as a little child will by no means enter it." And He took them up in His arms, laid His hands on them, and blessed them (Mark 10:13-16).

11

Picture yourself as a little child. You're tired, dirty from traveling dusty roads, trailing behind at the edge of the crowd. All day you've tried to keep up. Why are grown-ups always in a hurry?

Suddenly the constant movement of the crowd stops. As the mob presses in, there is anger, misunderstanding. You hear one Man's voice above the crowd, firm, but gentle. He is a warm and friendly man. He sits down under a tree to rest; the crowd backs away. Timidly, curiously, the children come forward and sit in a circle at His feet.

One by one, He picks up each boy, each girl, even the babies, and holds them in His lap. What would it be like to have Him hold you? You glance down at the dirt, a little afraid, uncertain. He may not notice you at all. And what if He does? Will you dare to go forward?

Just then, He looks your way and smiles. He stretches out His hand and invites you to come close. His hand is strong, tender, and you take it. You look up into His eyes. Soft, welcoming. . . The fear you felt earlier melts away.

He scoops you up into His arms. Relax. Lean back and rest your head on His broad shoulder. It feels so good just to rest. You didn't realize how tired you were. Tired. . . so tired. As you let go of your weariness, not just a physical weariness, but a frazzled feeling inside, a quiet strength seems to flow into you, a soothing peace.

Resting in Jesus' arms, you feel secure, protected. He tells you you are special, the apple of his eye. "_____ (insert your name), I love you. How precious you are. I love everything about you." He gently touches your nose, smiling at the freckles (which have always embarrassed you), stroking your hair (which you've always wished was blond or brown or curly like someone else's). Perhaps there is a scar on your face or a defect of some kind that you are ashamed of. No matter. Jesus loves you just the way you are. He tells you how much He loves you not only in words, but in the way He holds you, the way He looks at you.

Time seems to stand still. You are all alone with Jesus now. The crowd has gone. . . somewhere. Their voices hushed. You wish you could rest here forever. Perhaps there are tears. That's okay. Let them come. You don't know why you're crying. It's just that you've never been loved this way and you wish it would last.

Jesus knows your longing. "Come back," He smiles. "Come back often. Whenever you choose to return, I will be here. I will always be here for you."

And you know, because you have grown to trust Him, that His promise is true. You can return in prayer anytime, whenever you are feeling broken or empty or unsure of yourself or just tired. He will always be here to rest and restore you in His embrace. Always.[3]

Note: The prayer reflection above is taken from the audio cassette tape, *Healing Moments: Resting in God's Presence.* See page 113 to order a copy.

Questions for Group Discussion

1. Take some time in your group to share your prayer journeys. Have certain events or realizations catapulted you to different stages in prayer? Jot down any resources that have been especially helpful.

2. What is your greatest struggle in prayer? Do others in the group have suggestions about how to deal with this?

3. As a group try the prayer exercise on pages 11-14 together. Have one person read the Scripture; have another read the narrative while other group members close their eyes in prayer. After the reading, allow a minute or two of silence for everyone to think about what they've just heard. Then discuss your responses.

• Were you able to experience the presence of Jesus through this prayer?

• In what specific ways?

A Refreshing Place

When I woke up this morning, a delightful picture popped into my mind. I saw a tiny bird splashing in a birdbath. His little wings were flapping up and down playfully, and the water was dancing in cool droplets all around him. I have not seen a birdbath in a backyard for years. This was the kind I remember seeing as a child: a concrete bowl on a concrete pedestal, creating a small pool of water that gave a bird plenty of room to have a good time.

I smiled, imagining myself as that bird, splashing in the water without a care in the world. I felt rejuvenated, refreshed, an effervescent joy bubbling up inside me.

Oh, how I need moments like that. Too many times I wake up to the morning news on the radio. . . to a terrifying world, a world of sadness and tragedy. Add to this worries about my own world, concerns about the day, and sometimes I don't feel like getting out of bed at all!

Do you ever feel that way? Jesus said, "I came so they can have real and eternal life, more and better life than they ever dreamed of" (John 10:10 MSG).

What a promise! Yet how many of us experience life to its fullest, freest, most joyful? We are so pre-occupied with worries and concerns—some genuine, some needless—that our lives become burdensome, monotonous, full of despair. We desperately need a new infusion of energy to revive our zest for living.

This problem is not new. In Psalm 84, we see a picture of those who love God slowly making their way to worship at the temple in Jerusalem. It is an arduous journey; there are toils and hardships along the way, and they must pass through arid stretches. One such place is the Valley of Baca. The word *baca* in Hebrew means "weeping." You would expect to see somber faces as the pilgrims traverse this valley of tears. But that is not the case. Instead, the psalmist tells us, this hard, sad place is transformed into a "place of springs" and is "covered with pools of water" as the pilgrims are filled with joyful expectation of meeting God (v. 6).

Their sense of God's presence is so real it actually changes this dry wasteland into a place of refreshment, enabling them to "go from strength to strength" (v. 7).

This biblical story gives you and me great hope. It suggests that no matter how deep our valleys, no matter how difficult, we can find refreshment not only when we've made it through, but also right in the midst of these dry places. How can we draw on this hidden reservoir of strength in our own lives?

There is a "place of springs" accessible to us all. We find it when we find Jesus. "Come!" He says. "Whoever is thirsty, let him come and take the free gift of the water of life" (Revelation 22:17). This "water of life" that Jesus offers is like a perpetual spring welling up within us, providing an ever-renewable source of refreshment (John 4:14). We drink in this living water through prayer.

Entering Into Prayer

One of the reasons our lives become dry and empty is that we wander through a wasteland of busyness. We invest ourselves in things—houses, cars, and a host of other material possessions—which drain us of huge amounts of time and energy. Most of us are overcommitted and overextended, rarely taking the time to rest and restore our depleted energy. These pursuits often do not satisfy or fulfill us; they may even leave us feeling more empty than before.

How we need an oasis of rest! Prayer can provide a deep sense of rest that nourishes our bodies and souls. In prayer, we really can stop the world and get off. Whether we pray sitting in a comfortable chair in the living room or while walking in the woods or while gardening, it is good to relax, be still, and regain our equilibrium. Rest in itself is refreshing and revitalizing, but prayerful rest is more than that.

Remember the story of Mary and Martha, the two sisters who hosted Jesus in their home (Luke 10:38-42)? Each one responded differently to Jesus' visit. Martha was caught up in a whirlwind of activity; Mary chose to sit quietly at Jesus' feet and focus wholly on Him. As a result, Martha was snappy, resentful and short-tempered; Mary was calm and content. Which would you rather be?

Rest is a posture, an inward attitude, which allows us to be open and receptive to the Spirit of God. To truly enter into prayer, we need to make a conscious decision as Mary did to turn *away* from our compulsive busyness and turn *toward* Jesus. This means setting aside time to focus wholly on Him.

I often find, however, that just setting aside time to focus on God does not always mean that my attention is completely focused on Him. My mind can still be distracted and my spirit closed. I have to create psychological space as well as physical space to welcome His presence. This requires care and deliberate intention.

To still my busy mind, I sometimes gaze out the window at an object of natural beauty, perhaps a stately evergreen or a lilac bud in spring that evokes awe and wonder. Other times, I sit by the window and feel the sun warming my face. Sometimes I let music wash over me, or I may spend some time in silence—relaxing, waiting, listening. All these exercises help me be more open to God.

In the previous chapter, I mentioned a friend who has trouble concentrating in prayer. She finds two things helpful. When she sits down to pray, she lights a candle as a reminder that Jesus is the light of her life. If it is a scented candle, it also reminds her of His "sweet aroma" (2 Corinthians 2:15). Secondly, when distracting thoughts crowd into her mind, she simply writes them down, which frees her mind to focus again on prayer.

Worship Woos Us Into God's Presence

For me the most effective way to be open to God is to enter into worship as I begin to pray. Worship is simply expressing love and reverence for who God is. It is putting *our* thoughts aside, *our* desires, *our* preoccupations and fixing our eyes on Him. As Joy Huggett writes, "We become aware of our need to de-throne self and enthrone Christ afresh."[1]

David was a man after God's own heart, and this was his greatest desire: "One thing I ask of the Lord, this is what I seek; that I may dwell in the house of the Lord all the days of my life, to gaze upon the beauty of the Lord and to seek Him in His temple" (Psalm 27:4). How do you do this?

In her book *Open to God*, Huggett tells the story of a parish priest who was intrigued by a peasant who slipped into his village church every day as he walked to and from work. He spent long hours there just soaking up God's love. The priest asked him what he said to God as he spent time there. "I say nothing to Him," the peasant replied. "I look at Him, and He looks at me. And we tell each other that we love each other."[2]

Above and beyond any urgent prayer request we might feel is crying out for an answer, we have a deeper heart cry: to love and be loved. Prayer is not only talking to God and listening to God, but also being *with* God—giving full expression to our love,

22

appreciation, and gratitude for who He is and allowing the fullness of His love to flow into us.

Worship woos us into God's presence. Meditate on a psalm to begin your prayer time. Let the words direct your mind to think about God's greatness, His might, His compassion, His love, vast and limitless. In the light of God's love, cares and worries that loom so large in our minds may suddenly seem smaller, more manageable. We cannot handle them, but God can. It is enough just to rest in His presence like a little child embraced by the strong, tender arms of a loving Father.

The wider we open our hearts to the Spirit of God, the more fully He can enter in. Our bodies can help us pray. You might rest your hands in your lap, palms up, to welcome God's presence, or kneel to increase your attitude of reverence and worship, or lie prone on the floor either on your back or face down with your head resting on your hands.

I have also discovered that dancing while listening to praise music releases my spirit to be more open to God. David danced to the Lord out of joy (2 Samuel 6:14), and so can we. Dancing to God is a free avenue of expression. . . something you do for yourself.

Think of it as singing in the shower, not performance. Let yourself go. Clap your hands or lift them up as you sway to the music. Release your *whole body* to be an instrument of worship!

David composed his psalms or "songs" on a lyre. We have the benefit of a rich repertoire of contemporary worship music composed by Spirit-filled musicians. My favorites are the *Hosanna! Music* series (especially *Hillsongs Australia* music), the *Vineyard Music* series, and the more traditional *Praise and Worship* series from Campus Crusade for Christ.

Along with praise and worship, it is good to come into God's presence with gratitude. "Enter His gates with thanksgiving and his courts with praise" (Psalm 100:4). Spend some time reflecting on all the good gifts God has given you and your loved ones, thank Him for His faithfulness, His amazing grace.

Personalizing Scripture

During prayer, God invites you to be present to Him, and He really wants to be present to you. He wants to speak to you, give you guidance, heal a hurt, fill you with hope, and refresh you with His love. He can do this through the living pages of Scripture. Have your Bible with you when you pray. It is your greatest resource.

In the story of the Samaritan woman who meets Jesus at the well (John 4:4-15), Jesus senses the woman's tiredness and emptiness and offers her "living water" that will satisfy her deepest thirsts. As she comes close to Jesus and drinks His love deeply into her spirit, it refreshes and enlivens her. She becomes a new woman!

We can be refreshed in the same way as we dip into the well of Scripture. The key to letting God's Word renew you is learning to personalize Scripture. For example, take the words Jesus spoke to the Samaritan woman:

> "If you drink the water that I give you, you will never thirst. But the water I give you will become in you a fountain of water springing up into everlasting life" (John 4:14).

Now read the verse again hearing Jesus speak these words personally to you. You might even insert your own name. "If you drink the water that I give you, _____ (say your name), you will never thirst." If you are going through a dry and barren time in your life, words like this can suddenly give you new hope.

The words in the Bible are not merely words. They are God-breathed (2 Timothy 3:16), alive and full of power (Hebrews 4:12). The Spirit of God can activate any part of Scripture at any time and apply it to your life in a surprising way. Certain words or phrases seem to jump out at you or touch you more deeply than others. It may seem that God is speaking those words directly to you. He probably is!

Several years ago I faced a difficult crisis. I needed to find a job to help bring in more income. As I prayed about the situation, God seemed to be reassuring me that He would meet our financial need. This reassurance came through a specific verse, Philippians 4:19: "My God will meet all your needs according to his glorious riches in Christ Jesus."

I wanted to be reminded of that promise often, so I taped the verse on the steering wheel of my car. When I stopped at a red light or waited in traffic, I would glance at this verse and hear God say to me, "Betsy, I will meet all your needs according to my riches in Christ Jesus." This verse became a lifeline as months dragged on and nothing materialized. I have to admit there were times when I shot some words of my own back to God: "Okay. I've been praying, trusting. . . where's the answer?!" Finally, at the eleventh hour, our needs were met, gloriously I might add. I left that verse on my steering wheel for weeks afterward as a reminder to thank God for the way He met that need in spite of my fickle faith and utter despair.

"Prayer and the Bible go together," writes Jack Taylor. "Without the Bible prayer has no direction. Without prayer the Bible has no dynamic."[3] The Bible is the primary way God communicates with us. As you learn to hear God speak to you through the Bible, you will experience a vital, personal contact with God you may have never thought possible.

Prayer Walking

We've been talking about prayer being a refreshing place. Something *refreshing* is "pleasantly new and different, unusual." Are your prayer times pleasantly new and different? It is easy to slip into set ways of doing things. Our prayer times can become so stale and routine that we can go through the motions of prayer without communicating with God at all. I find that the more creative and fresh I make these times, the more they refresh me.

One of the most exciting ways I've learned to pray is prayer walking. My set routine used to be praying and reading the Bible at our dining room table. One spring day God seemed to draw me outside to experience Him in nature. A cedar deck wraps around our house, which is surrounded by lush, green woods. In the three years that we had lived there, I had never really taken the time to notice the beauty outside my window. Standing on the deck, I took several deep breaths, filling my lungs with fresh air and drinking in the sunshine like the newly budding leaves in the woods. As I did this, I was able to open my heart and take in the immensity of God's love in a way that I couldn't do indoors. Day by day, the woods and pond near my house became an inviting place of rest and refreshment in my busy life.

I often felt the tangible presence of Jesus as He walked beside me like a friend. During these intimate times of sharing, Jesus revealed things to me He could not tell me any other way. Once when I was walking through the woods, for example, I was feeling discouraged. I suddenly became aware of the quiet strength of the tall, straight elms all around me. I heard the words, "Stand tall in Jesus." Feeling their strength and hearing those words gave me a new confidence and inner strength, which I desperately needed at the time.

On some walks, there were no words. I simply felt a deep sense of peace as I let myself be immersed in the beauty and grandeur of God's creation. "In Him," Scripture says, "we live and move and have our being" (Acts 17:28). At these moments I felt completely at one with God.

Here are some suggestions to help you begin prayer walking:

- Allow 15 to 30 minutes for your walk. Later you might want to go longer.

- Stroll around a lake, through a park, the woods around your neighborhood.

- When you first launch out, don't think about a thing. Let your mind be at rest. Just enjoy getting outdoors. Let God draw your attention away from yourself to what He wants to show you.

- Listen to everything around you. . . and let Him speak to you.

- This is not the same as thinking about words on a page, purely a thought process. Let the whole world become your classroom. Open all your senses. Let God speak to your heart through what you see, hear, feel, observe.

- You can choose to begin or end your prayer time this way. Try to link your walk with Scripture that you are meditating on. The Holy Spirit will put two and two together in unexpected ways. Watch for startling connections, awesome new insights.

When the weather is bad and you can't go outside, don't let that stop you from prayer walking. Have a picture calendar nearby with large photographs of natural settings—gardens or mountain scenes or seascapes—whatever you enjoy. Imagine being in these tranquil settings as you pray. In the middle of winter, I love to imagine walking along a beach with Jesus as I look at a photograph of the ocean. I can even smell the salty air and hear the sound of sea gulls as I listen to environmental recordings of rolling surf.

Prayer walking is just one of many relaxing activities that is conducive to prayer. If you are a jogger, pray while jogging; if you enjoy fishing, pray as you fish. When I was a new mom, I had very little time alone to devote to prayer. I learned to pray while pushing my toddler on a swing in the backyard. I could easily sense Jesus standing next to me as I pushed her; I talked to Him quietly in my mind. These moments were so filled with the peace of God I believe my daughter was even aware of His gentle presence.

Find a way to pray that fits your lifestyle and suits the kind of person you are. But find a way to pray. An undercurrent of prayer flows just beneath the surface of your life. If it can be tapped, great blessings will flow forth.

One person of prayer put it well: "Looking back," he said, "my impression is that for many,

many years I was carrying prayer within my heart, but did not know it at the time. It was like a spring, but one covered by a stone. Then at a certain moment Jesus took the stone away. At that the spring began to flow and has been flowing ever since."[4]

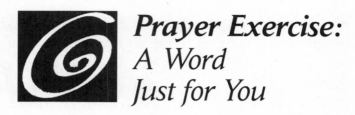

Prayer Exercise: A Word Just for You

Actually hearing God speak to you through the Bible may seem mysterious, even impossible. Let's try it. The verses below, which all center on the theme of being still, have been personalized—written as if God Himself were speaking these words directly to you.

Before reading these verses, take a moment to relax and get comfortable. Be completely still before God. Quiet your thoughts. So often we rush into prayer, anxious to tell God what is on our hearts and minds. This time simply rest in God's presence. . . and listen.

Meditate very s-l-o-w-l-y on these verses, phrase by phrase. Underline or circle key words or phrases that you are drawn to.

"Be still and know that I am God" (Psalm 46:10).
Who is at the center of your universe? You or God? Are you tired of holding up the whole world? "Here. Let Me carry it for a while," says the One who really does.

"Be still before the Lord and wait patiently for him; do not fret. . . " (Psalm 37:7-8).

Is there something you've been fretting about? Let go. . . and trust Me.

"The Lord will fight for you, you need only be still" *(Exodus 14:14).*

Are you in the midst of an overwhelming situation? Let Me do the fighting for you.

"Now then, stand still and see this great thing the Lord is about to do before your eyes!" *(1 Samuel 12:16)*

Is your God too small? Be still. Be expectant. See what I want to show you with the eyes of faith.

What did you hear? Think back over the words you've just read. Do some grab your attention more than others? Believe that they are God's own words meant for you here and now. (They are!) Linger on these words. Reflect on them in silence. Do they have any special meaning for your life? Write down what you think God is saying to you:

Respond to Him. In a conversation, one person responds to what another says. Take a moment now to respond to what God has said to you or shown you. In this space tell God what you are thinking or feeling. For example, if you feel encouraged, write a prayer of thanks. If God is directing you to take a specific action, write a prayer of commitment.

Questions for Group Discussion

1. Have you ever felt refreshed by prayer even when you've been going through a difficult time in your life?

2. Share your thoughts about what part worship plays in prayer. Perhaps for you it is only associated with Sunday morning when a congregation comes together to worship. Can you think of how you might incorporate it into your own prayer time? If you are familiar with this concept, share with the group effective ways that worship helps you enter into prayer.

3. Take 10-15 minutes to do the prayer exercise on pages 32-33 together. You might like to play some instrumental worship music in the background as you meditate on the Bible verses and listen to God speak to you. After you've allowed some time for silence and listening in prayer, ask your group, "Did God say or reveal something specific to you as you thought about these verses? Would you like to share these insights with everyone else?"

Chapter 3

A Healing Place

We often come to God in prayer, exhausted in need of rest, or weary in need of refreshment. We also come hurting in need of healing. Our prayers may not be eloquent. Sometimes we can't even put our thoughts into words. Instead we sink into silence and pour out our pain in tears. God draws especially close when we are hurting. "I have heard your prayer and seen your tears," He reassures us, "I will heal you" (2 Kings 20:5).

When we're hurting, we tend to be more open and vulnerable to God. One afternoon I took a prayer walk around the pond next to my house. I walked out my front door, strolled around the pond, and stopped to rest beneath a weeping willow. I sensed Jesus walking beside me like a friend;

He seemed especially close. A gentle breeze rustled the delicate fronds of the weeping willow that arched over my head. "When you weep," He whispered, "I weep with you."

These words moved me deeply because the pond was a place where I often let go of bottled up tears, pouring out my secret pain. I wondered how many times Jesus must have stood there watching me, entering into my pain, helping me bear it, even though I was not aware of His being there at all. What a profound expression of love that was, for often the pain of knowing we suffer alone is a wound in itself.

Prayer is a healing place. A place of solace and comfort, a place where you are never alone. "When you pass through the waters," the Lord promises, "I will be with you. . . they will not sweep over you" (Isaiah 43:2). "I will never leave you nor forsake you. . . I will be with you always" (Joshua 1:5; Matthew 28:20).

God Hurts to Heal

"God hurts to heal," wrote C. S. Lewis. He not only suffers with us, but He also longs to heal our hurts. How can we receive the comfort and healing we need through prayer?

To discover how God heals, start by opening the living pages of Scripture to see how He expressed

His love to hurting men and women through Jesus. "In the Gospels," writes Francis McNutt, "you see him spending a large part of the time going from one sick person to another, laying his hands on them and healing them. His heart goes out to people."[1] Jesus touched the blind and they could see, the crippled and they could walk. He reached out His hand in forgiveness to sinners, in peace to the fearful, in affirmation to the lonely.

At the end of Jesus' ministry, He commissioned His disciples to go into all the world and preach the Gospel. He promised that as they obeyed His command, miraculous signs would accompany their preaching, including healing the sick (Mark 16:18). At Pentecost, the Holy Spirit was poured out not only on them, but on all believers, men and women, young and old—for all generations to come (Acts 2:17). The Holy Spirit's power that was released in Jesus and those early believers is also a gift meant for us today.

Praying for healing, for ourselves and for others, can be a normal part of Christian life. You may think of healing prayer as mystical, beyond your reach, reserved just for those who have a special gift for such things, but I don't believe this is true. Just as Jesus said that faith as small as a mustard seed can move a mountain (Matthew 17:20), I believe that God responds to the prayers of ordinary people in extraordinary ways.

Stretch Out Your Hand

Jesus healed people in a variety of ways. His most common method of healing was the "laying on of hands." "The people brought to Jesus all who had various kinds of 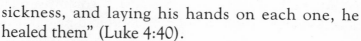 sickness, and laying his hands on each one, he healed them" (Luke 4:40).

In Acts 4:30, Peter and John asked God to "stretch out His hand" to perform healing miracles. God answered their prayer. As the apostles stretched out their hands in faith, people were healed, not because Peter and John had any special ability, but because God chose to let His supernatural power flow through their human hands.

"Stretch out *your* hand," God challenges you and me, "and see what happens." One night at dinner we were praying for my husband, who had an aching back. As we were praying, my ten-year-old daughter got up from her chair and put her arms around her dad as she prayed. Larry was so touched by this tangible expression of love that unexpected tears ran down his cheeks. His back, by the way, got better.

Brenna had learned to pray with touch because when she was sick, I would place my hand on her forehead and ask for the love of Jesus to flow into her body, filling her with His light and life. Even after her sickness waned, she would beg me to put my hand on her forehead and pray because she said, "It feels so good."

Touch is a wonderful way to express nurturing and love. It is the most natural thing in the world to hold a hand when someone is grieving, to soothe a child's crying with a hug, to touch the shoulder of a hurting friend to communicate compassion. God delights in using our hands to accomplish His divine intentions.

Years ago someone said some very wounding things to me. I was crushed inside. One morning at church a friend came up to me and said she was sorry about this injustice. Then she gave me a hug—a long, heartfelt, warm embrace. I felt God's compassion in her arms and nearly cried. The pain was instantly gone. I was amazed. "How could such a small gesture mean so much?" I asked God in prayer. "Her hug was bigger than your hurt," He answered.

What can happen in a moment? Everything if God is in it. God can use the smallest acts of kindness to bring healing to body and soul. He can also use our words.

Words That Hurt, Words That Heal

We all know the children's rhyme: "Sticks and stones will break my bones, but words will never hurt me." As we grow older, we learn just how untrue this is. Words *do* hurt. Harsh words can diminish our self-esteem and wound us deeply.

On the other hand, Scripture tells us that, "Pleasant words are a honeycomb, sweet to the soul and healing to the bones" (Proverbs 16:24). One of the most powerful ways God ministers to us is by pouring words of love like a healing balm into a wounded heart.

I remember praying for Phil, a middle-aged lawyer, who had never heard his father praise him. The only comments he heard growing up were angry put-downs that stung like a slap in the face: "You'll never amount to anything." "You're worthless." For years Phil believed these lies about himself. As I listened to his story, I thought of God's words to His son, Jesus, in Mark 1:11. Phil was God's son too. In prayer, I personalized the verse as if it were the heavenly Father's words spoken to him: "Phil, you are my beloved son in whom I am well pleased." As these affirming words penetrated his heart, Phil's face softened. His whole body seemed to relax. They had even greater effect as he learned to repeat them again and again to himself along with other biblical affirmations. As he did this, Phil distanced himself from the old, wounding words, and they lost their power over him.

You can speak words of affirmation and encouragement just as easily to your family and friends when they are hurting. Use your own words, or turn a Bible verse into a prayer. For example, you might personalize Psalm 103:11 this way: "For as high as the heavens are above the earth, so great is His love for you, _____ (name)."

You will be surprised by how healing words can be. They can soothe away the bumps and bruises of a hard day or infuse new hope into a crushed and tired spirit.

Healing Pain From the Past

Much of the hidden pain we deal with isn't on the surface of our lives. Its roots are buried in the deep recesses of our minds and spirits. Psychologists tell us that persistent emotional problems that have a strong hold on us—uncontrollable anger, compulsive fears and anxieties, a sense of worthlessness that we just can't shake—are often caused by patterns built up from past hurts. Unless these hurts are healed, they continue to sabotage our present and future.

Can pain from the past really be healed through prayer? Yes. Through a remarkable kind of prayer called "healing of memories." The idea of memory healing is to recall a painful incident in the past that still affects our present lives. Then in prayer we invite Jesus, who is the same yesterday, today and forever, to revisit the scene with us. His loving presence brings a warmth and light into the darkness of the memory that fundamentally transforms it.

The facts of the memory remain the same. The incident happened and that can't be undone, but the painful feelings associated with the memory, which still have power over us, can be released through prayer. Once we are free of the effects of a hurtful memory, we can move on with our lives in a healthy, constructive way.

Let me give you an example of memory healing. I prayed recently for a woman who had a destructive habit of putting up an emotional wall between herself and other people every time she was hurt. Through prayer we discovered that when Susie was ten years old, her parents had had a violent fight. Her mother stormed out of the house and said she was never coming back. Susie felt utterly abandoned and never safe again. This was when her wall-building began. In prayer we went back to that scene. Susie remembered the terror of that moment. However, this time she was aware of Jesus being there: His presence brought an inexplicable peace. Instead of anger in her parents' eyes, she saw

Jesus looking at her with love; instead of harsh screaming, she heard tender words of reassurance, "I will always be with you." And with that, He tenderly gathered her up in His arms and soothed away her fears. "I felt safe and rested," Susie remembers, ". . . the wall came tumbling down."

Susie was profoundly effected by this prayer experience. So much so that after this painful childhood memory was healed, she began to learn as a grown woman how to relate to people openly and honestly; she no longer hid from conflict. It would take time to develop new healthy habits, but Susie was on her way to making profound changes in her life.

There are three simple steps to memory healing. At the end of this chapter, you can try these steps and experience the healing presence of Jesus yourself or ask a close and trusted friend to pray with you. To learn more about memory healing, I suggest that you read my book, *The Healing Moment*,[2] or David Seamands' book, *Healing of Memories*.[3]

The Power of Forgiveness

When we are hurt, we are quick to blame someone else. It is our parents' fault, our offender's fault. . . even God's fault. Instead of fault-finding, the Bible says we need to forgive, no matter what the offense. Why? The obvious reason is that God tells us to, but there is another reason. Unforgiveness causes self-inflicted wounds.

"The man who broods over a wrong poisons his own soul," writes David Augsburger.[4] We are not responsible for what other people do to us, but we are responsible for our reactions. If we choose to hold on to anger, resentment, and bitterness, sometimes our sinful responses actually cause us more pain than the original hurt.

"If my years in the healing ministry have taught me one thing more than any other," says Cannon Jim Glennon, a well-known minister of healing prayer, "it is that nothing contributes more to sickness than resentment, and more to healing than to forgive. . . "[5]

Unforgiveness can make us physically and emotionally sick. We all know people whose sour countenances reflect a heart of bitterness, others whose backs actually bend under an invisible burden of resentment. Nursing negative feelings can cause recurring headaches, ulcers, depression, and a host of other maladies.

Forgiveness is a choice, not a feeling. We forgive, as Jesus teaches in the parable of the unmerciful servant (Matthew 18:23-35), because forgiveness is extended to us freely by a compassionate and gracious God and so in turn we offer it freely to others.

I have seen repeatedly that forgiveness has an incredible power to heal. One time when giving a talk on forgiveness, I gave small stones to everyone present. They were to hold the stones in their hands and not put them down even when taking notes or holding song books. It was awkward; the stones got in the way. In the same way, unforgiveness is a hindrance encumbering our lives. At the end of the class, I challenged everyone to think of someone in their lives they needed to forgive. Then I invited them to come forward and drop their stones in an empty bucket representing God's heart. God's heart is as deep as the deepest sea, and when we let go of our hard feelings toward someone, our sin is completely forgiven and forgotten.

Clack . . . clack. . . clack. Dozens of stones clattered in the bucket. A man with gray hair came up to me and asked if he could say something to the class. Hesitantly, I let him, though I felt uneasy, wondering if I had offended him.

"When I was five years old," he said, "my parents died and I was raised by my aunt and uncle. I hated them for fifty years; I was bitter toward God. Just last year I went back to visit my aunt and uncle. I asked them to forgive me for the resentment I had harbored toward them for so long."

Then he dropped his stone into the bucket. *Clack!* "I just want you to know," he said to the class with a smile, "this works. The bitterness and resentment are gone."

The Wounded Healer

There is a great deal of pain and injustice in the world. When contemplating suffering, our prayers should turn to Calvary, where the greatest injustice of all took place. "The world always has a different color, a different meaning, once you see it from the vantage point of the cross of Christ," writes Arthur Rouner. "The cross is about a price paid. The cross is about buying back all the dark and doubt and death of the devil—and giving the world a new start."[6]

Picture yourself standing at the foot of the cross with your hands open in prayer. It is here that we truly experience the deep, deep love of Jesus.

You can almost feel His tears falling into your open palms. "When you weep, I weep with you," He seems to intimate. "Will you weep with Me?"

It is here that the wounded healer longs to give you more of His heart. Will you weep over the sin and hurt in the world as He does, over those who still do not know His love and compassion? Will *you* become a wounded healer—one who is healed, yet still broken, one in need of prayer, yet one willing to pray for another's need?

Prayer is a healing place. A place where we enter into Christ's suffering and let Him enter into ours. A place where we begin to view the world in a whole new way.

Prayer Exercise:
Memory Healing

Scripture says that God can restore the years the locusts have eaten (Joel 2:25). Are there attitudes and behaviors that eat away at the positive things in your life? Perhaps memory healing can release you from that bondage. Let's try it.

Set aside a quiet time for reflection. Do not rush this exercise. Begin by coming into the presence of Jesus and feeling His deep love for you. Then follow these steps:

1. Ask the Holy Spirit to gently bring to mind a memory He wants to heal. It might be something that happened yesterday, or it might be something that happened years and years ago.

2. Once a memory comes to mind, the next step is to enter into the memory in prayer. Recall the scene as vividly as possible. What time of day is it? Who is there? What are you feeling?

3. Now picture with the eyes of faith Jesus actually being there. Can you sense the warmth of His presence? If you are a visual person, you may be able to see Him there. Where is He? What does He do? What does He say? As the incident unfolds,

Jesus will do what Love would do to heal the pain of the situation.

If there is need for forgiveness, add these two steps:

• If someone has hurt you, let Jesus stand between you and your offender so that the deepest woundings fall on Jesus—the angry words, the hurtful actions, any abuse. Let Him take the pain completely. "Surely he took up our infirmities and carried our sorrows. . . and by His wounds we are healed" (Isaiah 53:4-5).

• Part of the hurt you feel may be due to wrong attitudes on your part: anger, resentment, bitterness. Confess your own sinful attitudes and ask God to forgive you. Then ask the Lord to help you see the other person with His eyes of love and mercy. Can you forgive the person who has hurt you as God has forgiven you?

One step further: Take a few moments to think about what you've just experienced—a gift given to you in prayer. In the space on the next page try to capture what you learned through this personal prayer exercise by recording insights, impressions, or even drawing a picture of what you recall.

Journal your memory
healing experience.

Questions for Group Discussion

1. Can you think of a time when God used a small gesture of kindness to heal a hurt in your life? Write down a story to share.

2. Have you ever experienced healing prayer: having someone pray for you? What do you remember the most? Loving touch? Words that were said? Other feelings?

3. Have you ever prayed for someone else? What do you remember about that experience? What was the result?

4. Would you like to offer a healing prayer for someone in your group right now? Ask a volunteer to sit in a chair in the center of a circle. This is not a hot seat, but a *love seat*, where God wants to pour out His love to you through His Body, your brothers and sisters in Christ. Before the group prays, ask if the person has specific needs. If there is no particular need, the group should pray in whatever way God leads. Some of you may want to lay a hand gently on the person while you are praying (you might want to ask first). Take turns praying out loud. Use simple words of affirmation and encouragement or a Scripture verse that comes to mind. If you are not comfortable praying out loud, lend your support by praying silently in agreement with what is said. If there is time, invite others to sit in the love seat. You will learn a lot by letting people pray for you, then offering a prayer for someone else.

Chapter 4

A Transforming Place

Imagine yourself as a lump of clay, without shape or form. You are not very attractive. Nothing distinguishes you from the other lumps of clay sitting on the shelf. Then something happens. Strong, tender hands lift you from the shelf. You feel special just to be touched, admired. The Master Potter has plans for you. Good plans.

So He sets you spinning. Around and around. Slowly, slowly the wheel beneath you begins to move in a constant circular motion. The Potter's wheel vibrates with the steady rhythm of pumping feet that keep it turning. Faster, faster. . .

Whooaaa. . . You don't like being out of control in someone else's hands. These hands are changing you, and you don't always like change. Yet there is something in you, something deeper than you know, that responds to the warmth and purposefulness of these hands. They seem to know you even better than you know yourself.

The rough, brittle edges of your heart become soft and flexible as the Potter gently drips water onto your surface. This makes the clay workable as the water of the Word, of the Spirit, makes you responsive to the touch of Jesus.

> *Spirit of the living God, fall afresh on me*
> *Spirit of the living God, fall afresh on me*
> *Melt me, mold me, fill me, use me. . .* [1]

Your resistance to the Potter's hands melts as you yield to His love. With great care, He begins to shape a space in the center of your being. A rush of warm air, a light and gentle breath, sweeps into that inner space cleansing, refreshing, filling you up with new thoughts, new desires. *Melt me, mold me, fill me, use me. . .*

Slowly, slowly the wheel stops turning. Is that me? You can hardly recognize yourself! Once a dull, shapeless lump of clay, you now stand tall, an elegant vessel fit for noble purposes.

The Potter smiles. He is pleased. "You are fear-fully and wonderfully made..." (Psalm 139:14).

To Pray Is to Change

Prayer is a transforming place. Just as a potter fashions a shapeless lump of clay into something beautiful and useful, so God has a purpose and plan for your life. That purpose is revealed through prayer little by little, day by day.

"To pray is to change," writes Richard Foster. "Prayer is the central avenue God uses to transform us."[2] If you come into the presence of God through prayer, fully yielded and open to the Spirit's working in your life, you cannot remain the same.

"Like clay in the hand of the potter, so are you in my hand..." (Jeremiah 18:6). Prayer is learning to rest in God's hand, being soft and pliable, mold-able. Are you receptive and responsive to God's Word? Submissive to His Spirit?

Often I'm not. I'm resistant rather than respon-sive; stubborn and willful rather than submissive. Yet prayer has a way of changing me.

Let me give you an example of how transforming prayer can be. One morning our family was in tur-moil. My children were overtired, tense, and in tears. My husband pointed out that it was my fault for not getting them to bed on time the night before. I was defensive and angry. "If I didn't have to put them to bed on my own," I snapped back, "maybe they *would* get to bed on time!"

An argument ensued. There were accusations . . . counter accusations. I felt overwhelmed emotionally. Now I was tense and in tears.

After the children went to school and Larry went to work, I sat down to pray. I still felt angry and upset, still in the middle of a storm. The Lord led me to this verse in the Bible: "He brought me out into a spacious place; he rescued me because he delighted in me" (Psalm 18:19). David wrote these words after God had delivered him from his enemies who surrounded him on every side.

David's words spoke very directly to my stressful situation. I felt surrounded by enemies too, not physical ones, but emotional ones: anger, impatience, anxiety, self-pity. I needed to be rescued and led out into a spacious place just like David. And that's what God did for me through prayer. He created a space where I could quiet my soul and settle my mind again.

First of all, I felt a sense of peace as I drew close to God in prayer, a peace that came from His presence, not my outward circumstances. Then from that quiet center, I began to see things as they really were: I had overreacted emotionally. Certainly

Larry could have been kinder, but I was at fault too. My contentious attitude stirred up strife rather than quelling it. I asked the Lord to forgive me for my self-centeredness, then He gently suggested some ways I could handle the situation better next time. Without prayer, I probably would have remained upset all day and been more angry that evening. I learned that God can rescue us from anything—even ourselves.

Whether you need to change a bad attitude that lasts a day or unhealthy patterns of living that have lasted for years, prayer can change you and transform you as nothing else can.

People in Process

Most of us think of prayer as a means to an end. We are results-oriented. We pray for a need to be met, something to be accomplished. God, on the other hand, is process-oriented. He is much more interested in what kind of people we are becoming as we pray. Are we more loving, more patient, less driven by self-interest? Are we developing the gifts He has given us? Are we becoming more Christlike?

The Bible calls this process of inner transformation "sanctification." I think of it as Jesus' love penetrating deeper and deeper into our hearts, liberating us to a greater and greater degree until we reflect God's glory and discover who He meant for us to be. "And we, who with unveiled faces all reflect the Lord's glory, are being transformed into his likeness with ever-increasing glory . . . inwardly we are being renewed day by day" (2 Corinthians 3:18; 4:16).

As we are being transformed into Christ's likeness, it may seem at times that we are progressing at a snail's pace toward this goal. "If God wants me to be just like Jesus, why do I still seem just like me?" Max Lucado asks.[3] One moment we make a deliberate choice to avoid temptation, the next we slip back into it without thinking. Our old habits stubbornly resist change, but be encouraged. God *is* at work in us day by day transforming our passions, renewing our thoughts (2 Corinthians 4:16). Change is gradual, but it is sure.

Renewing Our Minds

How does this process of transformation take place? First of all, Paul tells us, it is a mental process. "Do not conform any longer to the pattern of this world," he warns, "but be transformed by the renewing of your mind" (Romans 12:2).

As we grow closer to God through prayer, "we begin to think God's thoughts after Him: to desire the things He desires, to love the things He loves. Progressively we are taught to see things from His point of view."[4]

This is an inward work of the Spirit, but it often leads to outward changes. For example, as you begin to see things from God's viewpoint, you may begin to change your lifestyle. Are the books I read and the movies I watch pleasing to God? What about the music I listen to? Does it make me desire what He desires?

Most of us have grown so accustomed to the world's viewpoint that we are totally unaware of how much it saturates our thinking. Sergio Scataglini, an evangelist from Argentina, points out that if we went to buy bottled water labeled "98% pure, sparkling spring water," we might be satisfied to buy it—until we read the small print —"plus 2% sewage."[5]

God calls us to holiness—to be set apart from the world (1 Peter 2:9). Why is this 2% moral pollution so important? Because the Bible says that our actions flow from our thought life (Luke 6:45). It is not hard to understand how looking at pornographic material could lead to lust; how coveting material possessions could turn to greed.

Every day we have a choice. We can choose God's way or the world's way. The Bible actually calls it a choice between blessings and curses, life and death (Deuteronomy 30:19). As we wrestle with these choices, it may seem at times as if we are in the midst of a fierce battle. We are. See Ephesians 6:12.

In this battle of the mind, we have an indispensable ally—the Holy Spirit. I remember a friend telling me about his experience in a West Berlin bar. Joe was steeped in the homosexual lifestyle but was slowly coming to Christ. One day he was sitting in a dark and dingy bar that he had frequented for years. Suddenly it was as if a light bulb went on. "It was a numbing, crushing moment, a moment of illumination," he said. "I saw the shabbiness of my surroundings and how deceptive my lifestyle was. I knew that God wanted more for me." That 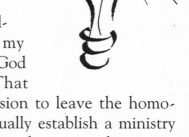 moment led to Joe's decision to leave the homosexual lifestyle and eventually establish a ministry to help others break free from homosexuality.

That insight came through prayerful reflection; the light bulb was the Holy Spirit. The Holy Spirit is called "the Spirit of truth" (John 14:17). When we pray, the Holy Spirit illumines our minds and helps us to see things from God's point of view.

He convicts us of sin, shows us the way out, and gives us the power to change.

I want to make an important distinction here. Conviction is not the same thing as condemnation. The Holy Spirit convicts us. Satan, our adversary who comes to "steal, kill and destroy" (John 10:10) condemns us. The Spirit of God is deeply grieved when we sin (Ephesians 4:30), but He has compassion for the sinner, encouraging us to right our wrongs and move on. Satan, on the other hand, attacks our self-worth by heaping condemnation on us: *you are worthless, hopeless, you will never conquer this weakness.*

Prayer is a welcome place—even when we have to face our own failings. There is no bludgeoning here, no shame. "There is no condemnation for those who are in Christ Jesus" (Romans 8:1). When you've sinned, Jesus says, confess it and I will cleanse you of all unrighteousness (1 John 1:9). You are forgiven completely and given a new start, not because of anything you can do, but because of what Christ has done on your behalf (Romans 8:1-2).

A Clean Heart

Transformation is a matter of the heart as well as the mind. After David had committed heinous sins, murder and adultery, he cried out, "Create in me a clean heart, O God, and renew a right spirit within me" (Psalm 51:10, KJV). David did have to suffer the consequences of his sin, but God in His infinite mercy restored the fallen king, and He will do the same for you and me.

Our hearts are highly deceptive. I learned this one day when I asked my seven-year-old to clean her bedroom. Carrie wanted to go to the park. "We'll go," I promised, "as soon as your room is clean."

Carrie dashed upstairs and returned in five minutes. "Come and see, Mom," she said, beaming. "It's as white as snow!"

Carrie's room did look spotless. It was only when I opened the closet door that her stashed-away-out-of-sight piles were discovered. Her attempt to make everything look right caused me to take a hard look at myself. "Isn't that what I try to do with God?" I reflected. "Stash my secret sins away while appearing to have a cleaned-up life."

God can't change our hearts until we know they need to be changed. That's why it is so important to spend some time in confession when we pray. After we enter into God's presence by exalting Him through praise and worship, we draw closer and become aware of His holiness. In the light of that holiness, we feel compelled to take off our masks and be honest: to see ourselves as we really are.

It is hard to admit our own neediness. But once we do, God can change us. "Oh, Lord," we pray, "I'm so sorry about the thoughtless way I wounded my friend. . . about giving into that temptation that always gets the better of me. . . about blaming others and slipping into self-pity."

Confess your lack of love, and God gives you *His* compassion; confess your weakness toward a certain temptation, and God gives you *His* strength to overcome it; confess your tendency to put yourself down, and God looks upon you with love and lifts you up. "I will give you a new heart," He promises, "and put a new spirit in you" (Ezekiel 36:26).

I realize this can take time. Some destructive tendencies in our lives are deeply ingrained. We can actually become enslaved to them. It may take a professional counselor or a friend more experienced in prayer to help us understand the root cause of a problem and deal with it.

But for the most part, if we are open and responsive to God, He will reveal what needs to be changed and help us make that change.

The Man Who Had No Face

Is there some aspect of your life you wish you could change? A secret addiction, an inner weakness, a destructive attitude? "I'll never change. That's just the way I am," you may tell yourself in despair. Let me share a story that illustrates how deeply transforming God's love can be. It will give you hope.

Years ago I met a man named Brian. Brian was an affable, middle-aged businessman, a husband and a father. He sang in the choir every Sunday at a Baptist church. Nobody guessed that Brian was contemplating suicide.

Brian's life was becoming more and more unbearable. He was filled with an overwhelming sense of inadequacy and self-hate. He had no solid sense of self; inside he simply felt emptiness. To fill this aching void he developed sexual addictions, which led to even more shame.

Like many wounded adults, Brian had suffered a lifetime of rejection. His father had been a "shadow figure," absorbed in his work, and his mother, abandoned by her husband, smothered Brian with a sick affection. Brian's parents had been too needy themselves to meet his own needs for love.

Desperate to stop his downward spiral of misery and pain, Brian came to me for prayer. For two years, he told me, he had been haunted by a disturbing dream. He saw a picture of a young boy wearing shorts and a T-shirt. His arms and legs were covered with festering, open sores like a leper.

His face was hidden by a white plastic hockey mask. Brian knew the dream was significant, but he didn't know what it meant.

God speaks to us in many ways: through words of Scripture, pictures, impressions, and dreams. I felt that this dream could be a key to Brian's healing.

It seemed to be a picture of how he saw himself—as a leper, unlovable, untouchable, ashamed to show his face. Until this picture of himself was changed, Brian would always see himself as rejected and worthless.

I sensed that God wanted to express His love to Brian as a nurturing parent, to restore the experience of unconditional love he had missed as a child. As Brian and I closed our eyes in prayer, I asked him if he could imagine the Gospel scene of Jesus holding the little children in His lap and blessing them (the prayer exercise in chapter 1). He had no trouble doing this.

Almost immediately, Brian saw in his mind's eye the boy with the leprous arms and legs and the mask on his face.

"Where is he?" I asked.

"Hiding behind a tree," Brian said. "Watching Jesus and the other children."

"Does he want to sit in Jesus' lap?"

"Yes," Brian said. "I wish He would choose me."

In prayer, Brian then saw Jesus reaching out His hand, inviting him to come close. Brian was hesitant at first, then slowly went forward. Resting in Jesus' arms, at last he felt the unconditional love and acceptance he hungered for.

I asked Brian to describe the boy now. "The wounds on his body are completely gone. His arms and legs are healthy, normal. He is just a wiry twelve-year-old boy like I was at that age."

I then asked him where the boy's mask was. "Gone," Brian said, suddenly surprised. "There's nothing there." He thought perhaps underneath the mask there would be wounds, but there was just nothingness. He had no face.

Then I asked Brian if he could see Jesus' face. Usually when people see Jesus' face in prayer, they see great love and affection, but this was not what Brian saw. Brian looked into Jesus' face and saw suffering. "His face looks tortured, in incredible pain, as He must have looked on the cross."

I explained that Jesus' suffering face must be reflecting Brian's own suffering. He began to sob, realizing how much Jesus understood his pain.

We waited in silence. Then the most amazing thing happened. Brian gasped and touched his own face. "My face feels like putty," he said. "Jesus is leaning down and putting His hands on my forehead, my nose, my cheeks. Like a potter molding clay." In awe, Brian described how carefully, slowly Jesus was making a new face for him. "He's giving me a new identity!"

As Brian's face changed, he saw Jesus' face change too. The pain and scars were gone; instead His face was joyous and strong, reflecting the inner transformation in Brian.

Then I spoke words to Brian that Jesus put in my heart for him: "Brian, I love you with an everlasting love. You are very, very special to me."

A big grin spread across Brian's face as he felt the power of those words flow into him. When we were finished praying, Brian was effusive. He could hardly contain his joy.

A couple of days later Brian told me a friend looked at him, astonished. "Brian," he said, "what happened to you? You have a new face!"

Was Brian's prayer experience just emotional and short-lived, or would it bring about a lasting change? Only time would tell. Destructive attitudes and habits need to be replaced by healthy ones; it takes time to learn new ways of relating and being. But knowing we are loved gives us the courage to begin that process of change.

Weeks after our prayer session, Brian wrote me with great gladness: "For the first time in my life, I have a center from which I can give and receive love."

A New Creation

Through prayer, Brian became a new creation. "Therefore, if anyone is in Christ," Scripture says, "he is a new creation; the old has gone; the new has come!" (2 Corinthians 5:17). The same thing can happen to you and me. The divine hands that fashioned us in our mother's womb are continually at work shaping and reshaping, bringing out the very best in us. This creative work is an ongoing process that lasts a lifetime.

"Like clay in the hand of the potter, so are you in my hand. . . " (Jeremiah 18:6). God can change you in ways you never thought possible. *Melt me, mold me, fill me, use me.* That is my prayer. Is it yours?

 *Prayer Exercise:*
Housecleaning

To renew your mind, I suggested becoming aware of the books you read, movies you watch, and music you listen to—things that subtly influence your thinking.

Take a prayer walk through your house. Ask Jesus to come with you. Look at your surroundings through His eyes. Walk into your family room. Are there any books, magazines, or videos that are sexually explicit, overly violent? Is the language questionable?

As you walk through your house, are the pictures on your walls peaceful or disturbing as you look at them with Jesus? Are they gateways for darkness or light?

You may have traveled to foreign countries and brought back souvenirs from other cultures. These may seem harmless, but they can have spiritual power. Do some research. What is the purpose of the object? Some of these things represent demonic spirits and can release darkness into your home.

Visit your son's or daughter's room. What books are they reading? Are there posters on the wall?

Look at their CDs. Read the lyrics. What values do they convey?

Finally, walk to your basement or garage, wherever you store keepsakes from the past. If you are married, are there love letters, gifts, or mementos from other serious relationships in your life outside of marriage? How does holding on to these things affect fidelity to your spouse?

Jesus is the Light of the world (John 8:12). Let Him be the Light of your world. After you have cleansed your house of unwholesome influences (this may mean throwing some things out), ask Jesus to fill each room of your house with His light, His purity, His power. Walk through the house again and pray His blessing into every room.

Questions for Group Discussion

1. Has God ever made you aware of a change you needed to make in your life? How did He do this? How did you respond?

2. Does holiness make you feel uneasy? Are you afraid of being called "holier-than-thou" by your family and friends?

3. As a group, discuss the "housecleaning" prayer exercise. Was it an eye-opener? Did it make you uncomfortable, or did it bring new freedom?

4. Share with your group one change you'd like to make in your life. As a group pray for one another, offering support and encouragement.

Chapter 5

A Partnering Place

As you allow God to mold and shape your life, to fill you and use you for His purposes, you begin to share the concerns of His heart—His desire to reach a lost and hurting world, His longing to wipe away tears, His yearning to mend the broken pieces of people's lives.

In the first chapter of this book, I described how my prayer journey took me to this place. Prayer became not just a way to talk to God and listen to God, but also an opportunity to partner with Him. As my heart was moved by His compassion, He seemed to be asking me, *Who will go to love and comfort and dry a tear?* Much to my surprise, I said, "Here I am. Send me."

What I did not realize is that God does not call us to do this alone. We are surrounded by a community of loving, enthusiastic men and women who are growing in their prayer lives too. They are hearing and answering the same call. "Here we are," the Body of Christ responds. "Send us!"

Just as Jesus sent out His disciples two by two, He calls us not only to partner with Him, but also to partner with each other as we do His work in the world. You may think of prayer as private, something you do in the solitude of your own heart. Certainly it is important to deepen your relationship with God through prayer, but I also want to challenge you to think beyond your own prayer closet to developing prayer partnerships.

Discovering the joy of praying with others can add a whole new dimension to your prayer life.

Two Are Better Than One

"Two are better than one, because they have a good return for their work," wrote the wisest man on earth (Ecclesiastes 4:9). This is certainly true when it comes to prayer.

Prayer partners can be a tremendous source of support and encouragement to one another. "Two are better than one. . . If one falls down, his friend can help him up. But pity the man who falls and has no one to help him up! Though one may be overpowered, two can defend themselves. A cord of three strands is not quickly broken" (Ecclesiastes 4:9-10, 12).

There are times when I face a struggle I cannot face alone. I may not even know how to pray. At those times it is so good to have a friend who can reach out and lift me up in prayer. Someone to offer a new perspective, a word of comfort or encouragement, a fresh infusion of energy as I run the race of life.

Prayer partners help lighten each other's load. That is what brothers and sisters in Christ are for. "We are members of one another" . . . "Carry each other's burdens, and in this way you will fulfill the law of Christ" (Ephesians 4:25; Galatians 6:2). The Body of Christ is a closely woven community in which we share our joys and sorrows, carry each other's burdens, and receive and give help when needed.

Prayer partners also hold each other accountable and strengthen one another. We all have weaknesses, those areas in our lives where we can easily be overpowered. "Every Christian has a weak side," says Stanley Tam. "That's where Satan always attacks. But if you have a prayer partner, your weakness will probably be your prayer partner's strength. The Bible speaks about one chasing a thousand, and two putting ten thousand to flight.

When you have a prayer partner, you become ten times stronger!"[1]

Is there more power in praying together than alone? Yes. I believe so. Not only for our own mutual support, but also because our prayers are more effective as we do battle for others.

The Power of Agreement

"If two of you on earth agree about anything you ask for," Jesus promised, "it will be done for them by my Father in heaven" (Matthew 18:19). This important prayer principle is known as the power of agreement. It takes love to agree and strive together toward a common goal, almost supernatural love at times. This releases supernatural power.

I experienced a dramatic example of this principle several years ago. One evening at about eight o'clock, I felt a strong leading from the Holy Spirit to pray for my friend Mary. I knew Mary struggled with depression and suicidal thoughts, and I sensed that she might be in serious trouble that evening. As it turned out, she was.

I called my prayer partner, a woman who had prayed with me for Mary many times. For about a half hour we prayed over the phone. There are times in prayer when you know that you are in the midst of a battle; this was one of those times.

We prayed against a heavy darkness that we felt was bearing down on Mary, a darkness we knew she could not withstand alone. "Lord," we prayed, using the strong name of Jesus and His authority, "we stand against the spirit of death and ask You to send Your light to dispel the darkness." Our own spirits felt heavy as we prayed. Then gradually as prayer did its work, we both felt the invisible burden lift. The battle was over.

Mary called me the next day and told me the strangest thing had happened. The night before she had been at a party at a neighbor's house. She was laughing and enjoying herself. Then for no explicable reason, she felt a dark cloud of depression weighing down on her. "It was *so* heavy," she said, "I felt miserable and didn't want to live. Then for some reason the dark cloud lifted. . . just lifted and went away."

I asked Mary what time this happened. She had just looked at her watch. It was eight o'clock.

Did our prayers make a difference? Without a doubt. Could I have prayed for Mary on my own? Yes, but I really don't believe my prayers would have had the same power.

Prayers of agreement are not only more effective, they are also more rewarding. When a request is answered, it is thrilling to praise God together!

Finding a Prayer Partner

How do you find a prayer partner? Prayer partners are special people. They become close friends and confidantes and spur you on to growth in your prayer life that you probably would not experience on your own.

There are certain qualities to look for in a good prayer partner. Do you know someone who enjoys prayer and has a hunger to grow in prayer as you do? Does he/she have an ability to listen to God? A willingness to keep confidences? Can you learn from each other?

While these qualities describe good prayer partners in general, I also look for specific partners for specific prayer tasks. For example, if I need prayer for my marriage, I find someone who needs prayer for her marriage too. Because we share the same need, we can pray with and for each other with greater understanding, depth, and compassion.

Also in looking for a prayer partner, ask yourself, "What do I feel passionate about?" Passion fuels fervency in prayer. If you have a longing to see revival in your church, God has probably put that same longing on someone else's heart. Partner with that person, and you will double your effectiveness. If you want to reach your neighborhood for Christ, find a neighbor to pray with who shares that same desire.

A Welcome Place for Partners

Just as prayer can be a welcome place for you to grow close to God, it can also be a welcome place for partners to grow close to God together. But for a partnership to work well, both partners need to be mutually hospitable to each other.

For example, you might find a prayer partner who shares the same passion in prayer, but you may have different levels of prayer experience. One of you may be very comfortable praying out loud, while the other has never done this before. To help the less experienced partner feel more confident, the more mature partner can let the other person pray first, which avoids the problem of "grand-standing," covering everything in one long-winded prayer.

Praying in agreement also requires a cooperative spirit. After the other person has prayed first, listen carefully and add some of your own thoughts to strengthen or reinforce what was said instead of being preoccupied with what you are going to say next. In this way prayer flows back and forth, moving broader and deeper in the same direction, rather than wandering aimlessly from topic to topic.

One of the greatest benefits of praying with a partner is learning new prayer styles. One person may think visually. As soon as a situation is mentioned in prayer, God reveals insights to that person in the form of pictures. While praying about the same situation, another person may hear what God says. That person will probably have a Scripture verse come to mind.

Rather than being limited to one way of praying, stretch yourself. Try something new. After your partner prays in a particular style, follow that lead and try it too. In time you will become more proficient in new methods, which will enrich the way you already pray.

Prayer partnership is an intimate relationship. As a rule, I would suggest that a man and woman do not pray together privately on a regular basis. However, it is wonderful for a husband and wife to pray together. Sadly, very few Christian couples do this.

Why? Prayer is so intimate it can be intimidating. A husband may be afraid to be honest and vulnerable with his feelings; a wife may be self-conscious about not saying or doing the right thing in prayer. But can you imagine two people who have more common concerns than marriage partners: raising children, career decisions, unexpected life crises? Even though it may seem awkward at first, barriers to praying together can be overcome, and it is well worth persisting. "A couple praying together will see God do wonderful and powerful things," says Larry Keefauver, who has written an excellent book to help couples build prayer partnerships.[2]

Prayer Groups

Prayer partnerships are not limited to two people. They can also be groups of people or teams brought together for a common purpose. You can be part of a church prayer group that prays for the needs of your congregation, or a Bible study group of friends or neighbors, or a healing ministry team that prays for hurting people.

Being part of a prayer group or ministry team is a great way to grow in prayer. "There are different kinds of gifts," says Paul, "but the same Spirit" (1 Corinthians 12:4). Each of us is unique. We have different natural and spiritual gifts. These gifts only operate in full power when they are functioning together under the leadership of the Holy Spirit in the Body of Christ.

It is in the context of the Body that we learn what our gifts are and how they can best be used. Prayer groups provide a supportive atmosphere where you can receive helpful feedback and begin to understand how your specific gifts work most effectively with others to accomplish God's purposes.

I remember years ago leading a prayer group for the first time. God had given me a specific verse to help focus our prayer time. Three people had been given the same verse! I came to understand how valuable it was to pray with others rather than alone. As we prayed together, every word that was said, every insight given, seemed to blend beautifully like different instruments in an orchestra playing the same piece of music.

God Blesses Unity

Prayer has a remarkable way of uniting people—not only groups of individuals in the same room, but also whole churches and whole communities. "How good and pleasant it is when brothers and sisters live together in unity!" proclaims the psalmist. "For there the Lord bestows His blessing, even life forevermore" (Psalm 133:1, 3).

We live in exciting times. Prayer movements across the country are springing up in city after city, bringing together people of different races, denominations, all walks of life to pray for their cities, their country, the world. Praying with a large, diverse group of Christians will allow you to become involved in the grand, sweeping purposes of what God is doing today.

Do you want to experience extraordinary power in prayer? Find a partner to pray with on a regular basis, join a prayer group, or become part of a broad-based prayer movement.

A single instrument can make a beautiful sound, but how much richer and fuller it is when combined with a whole orchestra!

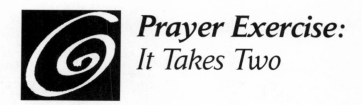

Prayer Exercise:
It Takes Two

After reading this chapter, I hope you are eager to establish a prayer partnership with someone. Here are some questions to ask yourself as you begin to think and pray about finding a prayer partner:

• What do you feel passionate about? List three things that really move you to pray. Perhaps you have concerns that you have prayed about on your own, but you sense that extra prayer power is needed.

• In looking for a prayer partner, what are the qualities that matter most to you? Jot down some specifics.

• If you could pray together with someone, how often would you want to meet? What day? Time of day? Is there a specific place that would work best for you?

• Write down the names of people who are potential prayer partners.

Pray over this list, then ask God to show you how you can invite this person to become a prayer partner.

Questions for Group Discussion

1. What are some of the benefits of praying together, not just on your own? You may think of examples mentioned in this chapter, or you might want to add some insights from your own experience.

2. What are some of the barriers to praying together? Can anyone in the group offer specific suggestions to overcome these?

3. What have you enjoyed the most about praying together in this group?

4. Carrying one another's burdens is one of the
great benefits of prayer partnerships. Let's take time
to practice that now. Have your group divide into
pairs. Facing each other, have one person extend
his/her hands to the other as if they are Jesus'
hands. Holding your hands palms up, say to that
person as Jesus would, "Cast your cares upon Me
because I care for you" (1 Peter 5:7). The person
with the burden should imagine holding a heavy
rock. Spend a few moments in prayer with your
eyes closed, thinking about what that burden might
be. Then hand the rock over to your partner as if
truly letting it go into Jesus' hands. You might say,
"Lord, I give you _____"
(name something specific) or say generally, "all
my worries and concerns." When this is expressed
out loud, the other person should speak words
of encouragement or release as Jesus would.
You might want to personalize a Scripture verse.
Some suggestions:

If a worry is acknowledged:

Don't be anxious about anything, _____ (use the person's name), but in everything by prayer and petition, with thanksgiving, present your requests to God. . . and He will give you His peace, a peace which transcends all understanding (Philippians 4:6-7). Receive His gift of peace.

If a sin is confessed:

_____ (use the person's name), the Bible says, "If we confess our sins, he is faithful and just and will forgive us our sins and purify us from all unrighteousness" (1 John 1:9). In Jesus' name receive the gift of His forgiveness.

If fear is expressed:

God hasn't given you a spirit of fear, _____ (use the person's name), but a spirit of power and of love and of a sound mind (2 Timothy 1:7, NKJV). Receive these gifts; they are yours, _____.

After you have prayed in this way, exchange roles. Let the giver be the receiver.

Chapter 6

A Liberating Place

Prayer is a place in our hearts where we meet God. A place where we can truly relax and be ourselves, where we are refreshed, healed, transformed. . . and set free.

Remember the image at the beginning of this book? Prayer was pictured as a cozy living room, warm and relaxing. As you come home weary and exhausted from a hard day, you are greeted by a loving Friend. He lifts the burdens from your arms and invites you to sit in a comfortable chair. "Tell me about your day," He smiles. In the company of this close and trusted Friend, you feel free to share your deepest feelings. You feel understood, cared for, completely at ease.

Prayer is like that, wonderfully restful, but that is not all it is. Little by little as you visit with Jesus, your familiar surroundings may begin to change. Where there was once a solid wall, now a window appears, and perhaps in time a whole wall is demolished. The world outside your window comes closer than ever before. You may begin to notice your living room grow visibly brighter as skylights are put in. An open heaven above affords a broader, more expansive view, beyond anything you might have imagined.

"Enlarge the place of your tent." Those words, God-breathed, full of surprise, begin to take hold in a mysterious way. "Stretch your tent curtains wide, do not hold back; lengthen your cords, strengthen your stakes. For you will spread out to the right and to the left. . . " (Isaiah 54:2-3a).

Yes, prayer enlarges your heart. It stretches you and broadens you—sometimes beyond your comfort zone—but this is not a bad thing because feeling a fresh breeze waft through an open window can be refreshing, and letting more light into your life brings the joy of new possibilities.

Where the Spirit of the Lord Is, There Is Freedom

"If anyone loves me," says Jesus, "My Father will love him and we will come to him and make our home with him" (John 14:23). When we accept Christ into our lives, He dwells within us: He is always there to welcome and nurture us. He is also there to release us to grow beyond the bounds of who we are.

Spiritual growth may seem unsettling, and it can be at times, but Scripture promises that "where the Spirit of the Lord is, there is freedom" (2 Corinthians 3:17). It is the Spirit within us that causes us to let the walls come down in our hearts, to let God stretch us in new and unexpected ways.

I remember once enjoying a wonderful, relaxing prayer time in my living room. Sunlight flooded in the room, filling me with a deep sense of peace. All was well with the world until a knock on my front door suddenly shattered the quiet of that moment. "Who can that be?" I wondered, a bit perturbed.

I was surprised to find a close friend standing on the doorstep. She was distressed and shaking, with tears running down her face. "I didn't know where else to go," she said apologetically.

I invited her in and listened as she told me the terrible news that her teenage son had run away. She was a single mom, and this boy—rebellious, wayward, on drugs—meant everything to her. She was beside herself with fear. A knife had been taken from the kitchen, a suicide note found.

The next two days were sheer terror for this fragile mother as the police launched a nation-wide search and high school students combed deserted woods for signs of their missing classmate. I sat with my friend as a dark night of the soul engulfed her, sharing her anguish, holding out hope when there was none. Then, as unexpectedly as the boy had disappeared, he showed up again at home. Fear gave way to great rejoicing.

How could I have guessed what I would find when I had opened the door two days before? I certainly did not expect to step into an intense life and death drama. However, I suspect that God knew. For what good would prayer have done if it had been kept in the confines of my own living room? Did God pour peace into me that morning just for my own enjoyment, or to calm a troubled soul that desperately needed that peace far more than I did?

Would you have opened the door? Would you let a friend in need disturb the tranquility of your prayer time? I believe you would. Prayer empowers us to do things we wouldn't do otherwise: to embrace others as we have been embraced, to freely give as we've freely received out of the overflow of God's lavish love for us.

Where the Spirit of the Lord is, there is freedom. . . prayer is a liberating place.

On a different occasion when I was praying in my living room, I read in the Bible how the early apostles had stretched out their hands in faith in the name of Jesus and people were healed miracu-lously (Acts 4:30). My heart was stirred by a long-ing to be used that way too. "Why can't I do that?" I cried out to God.

At that exact moment the phone rang. A woman whom I had met a year ago at a conference said that she had been trying to get hold of me ever since I had prayed for her that day. Vaguely, I remembered a middle-aged woman with an injured leg. She had asked for prayer because she had no insurance and could not afford to go to the doctor. With very little faith and thinking to myself that she was crazy not to seek medical treatment, I stretched out my hand and prayed for Jesus to heal her leg.

"I just wanted you to know," said the woman, "that my leg was completely healed after you prayed for me. I walked down the stairs without pain the next day. I even ran around the house! That was a year ago. It's still fine."

I was stunned, not only by what she said, but by the timing of the call. I have rarely experienced such an unmistakable answer to prayer.

If you were asked to pray for someone's healing, would you stretch out your hand in faith, even lit-tle faith, and offer to be used by God? I believe you would. We reach out in the name of Jesus, in our weakness, in His strength, and miracles happen.

Where the Spirit of the Lord is, there is freedom. . . prayer is a liberating place.

Just Say Yes!

When I am faced with caring for someone in need or stretching out my hand in faith, I find a simple exercise sometimes helps me get over my sense of inadequacy, my fear, my self-centeredness, or whatever else holds me back.

The Bible tells us to "lift up holy hands in prayer" (1 Timothy 2:8). If you stand and lift up your hands above your head in an attitude of praise and worship, you will notice that your body forms a "Y"—the first letter of the word, "yes." It is a powerful prayerful posture of submission, of opening ourselves to God's direction, of utter yieldedness. We say with this gesture:

Yes, God, use me.

Yes, Lord, I'm available.

Yes, Holy Spirit, flow through me.

When we pray this prayer, God does use us. Amazing answers to prayer may happen when we least expect it.

Tim was sitting in his second grade classroom when God called him to pray for a friend. When Tim turned in his math paper that morning with only two problems on it, his teacher accused him of not paying attention in class. His mother was angry too. "Were you daydreaming?" she asked. "Goofing around?"

"Mom," Tim explained, "I was praying for Simon. I had this feeling that he was going to die, and I needed to pray for him right then."

Tim's mother was taken aback. Simon was a struggling premature baby who had been in the hospital for weeks. His picture was on their refrigerator at home, and she had encouraged her children to pray for the baby, the son of a family friend.

Tim's mother suggested that they call Simon's mother. Simon's mother was very surprised by Tim's call. She asked him what time his math class was when he felt led to pray.

"Ten o'clock," he said.

The second grader's eyes grew wide as saucers when she told him that Simon's lung had collapsed at ten that morning and he nearly died.

Tim was awestruck. "Why did God pick me?" he asked his mother. She smiled with tears in her eyes. "You were given a special assignment, Tim. Other people probably were too busy to pray, or maybe they just don't hear God like you do."

That incident turned Tim into a passionate intercessor. He prays often for family and friends now. "God listens to me when I pray for sick people," he says.

Tim is an intercessor. "A what?" he might ask. I'm sure this ten-year-old has never read a book on intercession or attended a seminar on the subject. Unlike so many of us who feel we have to be highly skilled at prayer or have tremendous faith, Tim simply says:

Yes, God, use me.

Yes, Lord, I'm available.

Yes, Holy Spirit, flow through me.

And He does.

You Can't Outgive God

Abraham said yes to God. He was asked to build an altar and sacrifice his only son, Isaac (Genesis 22:1-18). As he lifted the knife to kill Issac, God stopped him and provided a ram instead for the offering. Abraham did not have to sacrifice his son, but he showed God that he was willing to give up anything that God asked of him. As a result of Abraham's obedience, he not only saved his son, but he was also blessed beyond measure.

Saying yes to God often involves sacrifice. This may mean giving up your plans for a day to serve someone else. It may mean reaching out your hand in faith when you feel foolish. It may mean surrendering something much bigger: a relationship, fixed expectations, dreams and ambitions.

Years ago I was faced with this challenge. A close friend of mine said, "I think you need to put your writing on the altar." She was referring to the story of Abraham. I was stunned. I loved God, but giving up my writing career was unthinkable. It was my life, my identity. My friend reassured me, "If you do this, it will be returned to you a hundredfold."

I wrestled in prayer with what she said for some time. Then one day I asked God, "If you want me to give up my writing, is there something else you want to develop in me?"

In my mind's eye, I saw the word "TEACHING" in big letters on a blackboard.

Teaching was the last thing I wanted to do with my life! Much to my surprise a few weeks later I got a call out of the blue asking if I would teach journalism at a nearby college. I took the job and couldn't believe how much I enjoyed teaching.

I took my friend's advice and "put my writing on the altar." I did not publish for ten years. During that time, God developed a multitude of other gifts in me—teaching, healing, counseling, discipling, pastoring—that gave me even more joy than writing.

The altar has become a permanent fixture in my prayer life now. God often calls me there. It is a place of wrestling, a place of letting go, a place of boundless growth. One day I felt led by God to put my shoes on a footstool in my living room, thinking of it as an altar.

"Are you willing to go where I lead you?" God asked as I looked at my shoes.

It was a hard question. "Where?" I wanted to know. "When? For how long?" There were no answers; it would not be faith if I knew. The question remained: "Are you willing to go where I lead you?" After some penetrating soul searching, I said yes.

If faced with a similar challenge, with a question of obedience, of surrender, would you say yes? I believe you would because prayer is a liberating place. It allows you to do the unthinkable—to lose your life so that you can embrace something far greater.

"Give away your life," Jesus said. "You'll find life given back, but not merely given back—given back with a bonus and a blessing" (Matthew 10:39, MSG).

A Bonus and a Blessing

What is the bonus and the blessing Jesus promises? For each of us it is a different unexpected joy. For me it has been the thrill of seeing other people set free as I have been set free through prayer.

At the end of a retreat, I once challenged 120 women to put their shoes on the altar as an exercise of faith. We used a piano bench as an altar with two tall candles on it. I put my shoes on the bench first, then invited the women to come forward and put their shoes on the altar to represent a step of faith God might be calling them to at that moment.

I wondered if anyone would come forward. It might be embarrassing to carry your shoes in your hand and walk up an aisle. What would your friends think? Wouldn't you look foolish . . . feel foolish?

Quiet music played while I asked everyone to search their hearts, then come forward if they wished. I closed my eyes in prayer and waited. When I opened my eyes, I could hardly believe what I saw! My single pair of shoes was suddenly surrounded by a sea of shoes. They covered the piano bench and spilled over onto the floor many rows deep—more than a hundred of them, all shapes and sizes.

One pair of shoes represented a woman who surrendered her life to Christ for the first time. Other shoes belonged to women who felt called into new ministries; one made a commitment to go into missions. Still others made commitments to reach out and mend broken relationships, or to walk back into difficult family situations.

I recognized some of the shoes on that altar. They were worn by people I had prayed for, some struggling with deep hurt, and yet they had come forward in a step of faith. These women had been healed, filled with hope, emboldened. As one said, "God has asked me to jump into tomorrow with both feet and I've said yes!"

Prayer is a liberating place. It sets us free to expand our faith and care about the hurting world around us, to take risks we would not take otherwise. "Give away your life. You'll find life given back, but not merely given back—given back with a bonus and a blessing."

My hope is that this book has set you free to expand your vision of prayer, introduced you to some new, exciting ways to meet God, suggested ways to partner with others in prayer, and finally inspired you to enlarge your heart to reach out to others.

May you discover the blessing that Jesus promises as prayer propels you forward into a lifetime of service and ever-increasing joy.

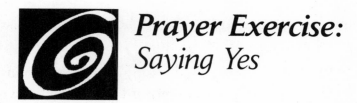

Prayer Exercise: Saying Yes

For this last exercise, find a place in your home where you can stand and face the world outside. Open your hands in prayer, lifting them above your head in an attitude of praise and worship. You might like to play praise and worship music as you do this. Be aware of your body forming the shape of a "Y," the first letter of the word "yes."

As you open your hands in praise, direct your thoughts upward and outward to God. Open your heart as well. Gaze up at the sky and think about God's greatness—the width, the breadth, the depth of His love for you.

Take a deep breath. In the Bible the Holy Spirit is called the *pneuma*, the breath of God. Imagine breathing in the expansiveness of God's Spirit. Feel the cleansing, polishing breath of the Spirit flowing through your body. Let every muscle, every tissue, every cell breathe it in.

How do you say yes to God? Let go of what is in your hands; let go of what is in your heart. . . and simply let Him fill you with Himself. As you say yes, God says yes to you: "No matter how many promises I have made, they are 'Yes' in Christ" (2 Corinthians 1:20). Recite some of those promises now:

Yes, I can do everything through him who gives me strength (Philippians 4:13). Let His strength infuse you as you say those words.

Perfect love drives out fear (1 John 4:18). Yes . . . Let His love melt away any fear.

If the Son sets me free, I am free indeed (John 8:36) Yes . . . Rejoice in that freedom.

"Yes! Yes!" Shout it to the universe with your arms opened wide. Whisper it in awe.

Yes. Yes. All my yeses are found in Jesus.

Questions for Group Discussion

1. In this chapter I mentioned two specific instances where I was stretched by prayer: having a tranquil prayer time interrupted by a friend in need, and being asked to pray for someone's healing. Discuss one or both of these experiences, imagining yourself in that situation.

2. As a final group exercise, ask your group to sit in a circle with a chair, bench, or footstool in the center of the circle. Think of this as an altar. Prayerfully listen to some music, then wait in silence, asking God if there is a step of faith He wants each of you to take today. When you know what that is, place your shoes on the altar.

Share with the group the step of faith each of you was challenged to take. Pray for one another, asking God for guidance, strength, and perseverance as you follow through on these commitments.

Notice the shoes placed together on the altar. Think about how different they are and how unique each member of your group is. In the Body of Christ, we never step out alone. We step out together. Make a commitment to uphold one another in prayer as you move on from this group.

3. Conclude your time together by giving each other a prayer of blessing. Someone can begin by blessing the person on the right, then that person in turn can bless the person on his/her right until everyone in the circle has been blessed. Pray God's best for that person. As you say the blessing, you might also lay your hand lightly on your friend's shoulder or put you hand on his/her head to let God's love flow through you as you speak. Some suggested words of blessing:

Lord, Jesus, I ask you to bless _____. Pour out the oil of gladness on her life. Release every gift, every talent, every good thing in _____ that she might be a delight to You and to others. Lord, when she is weak, may You be her strength. When she needs guidance, give her wisdom. When she is discouraged, give her hope. May she know, Lord, how deeply you love her and how closely You walk with her every day. Amen.

Notes

Chapter 1

1. Betsy Lee, *Miracle in the Making* (Minneapolis, Minn.: Augsburg Publishing House, 1983).

2. Jack Taylor, *Prayer: Life's Limitless Reach* (Nashville, Tenn.: Broadman Press, 1977), p. 19.

3. Betsy Lee and Michael Pearce Donley, *Healing Moments: Resting in God's Presence* (Bloomington, Minn.: Prayer Ventures, Inc., 1996).

Chapter 2

1. Joyce Huggett, *Open to God* (Downers Grove, Ill.: Intervarsity Press, 1989), p. 34.

2. Ibid., p. 26.

3. Jack Taylor, Op. cit., p. 111.

4. Joyce Huggett, Op cit., p. 20.

Chapter 3

1. Francis MacNutt, *The Prayer That Heals* (Notre Dame, Ind.: Ave Maria Press, 1981), p. 16.

2. Betsy Lee, *The Healing Moment* (Nashville, Tenn.: Thomas Nelson Publishers, 1994).

3. David Seamands, *Healing of Memories* (Wheaton, Ill.: Victor Books, 1985).

4. David Augsburger, *The Freedom of Forgiveness* (Chicago, Ill.: Moody Press, 1960), p. 14.

5. Jim Glennon, *How Can I Find Healing?* (South Plainfield, N.J.: Bridge Publishing, Inc., 1984), pp. 43-44.

6. Taken from a sermon by Arthur A. Rouner, Jr., "Picking It Up," in the "Way of the Cross" Lenten Series, preached at Colonial Church, Edina, MN, March 5, 1992.

Chapter 4

1. Daniel Iverson, "Spirit of the Living God," (Nasvhille, Tenn.: Birdwing Music). All rights reserved. Used by permission.

2. Richard Foster, *Celebration of Discipline* (San Francisco, Calif.: Harper & Row Publishers, 1978), p. 30.

3. Max Lucado, *Just Like Jesus* (Nashville, Tenn.: Word Publishing, 1998), p. 8.

4. Richard Foster, Op. cit., p. 30.

5. Taken from a message by Sergio Scataglini given at "Light the Nation" Conference in Dallas, Texas, May 7, 1998.

Chapter 5

1. David Mains and Steve Bell, *Two Are Better Than One: A Guide to Prayer Partnerships That Work* (Portland, Oreg.: Multnomah, 1991), pp. 7 - 8.

2. Larry Keefauver, *Lord, I Wish My Husband Would Pray With Me: Breaking Down the Spiritual Walls Between You and Your Husband* (Orlando, Fla.: Creation House, 1998), p. 169.

About the Author

Betsy Lee is an author, speaker, and president of Prayer Ventures, a ministry that provides retreats and resources to help people grow in their prayer lives.

She has written several books, including *The Healing Moment* and *The Legacy of the Blessing* with John Trent and Gary Smalley.

Betsy has been involved in prayer ministry for fifteen years: working one-on-one with wounded men and women, training prayer teams, teaching seminars, and leading retreats. "My greatest joy is communicating the love of Jesus in fresh and creative ways," says Betsy. "Every session I teach is bathed in prayer, allowing the Spirit of God to minister deeply to the personal needs of everyone who attends." To find out more about hosting an event, contact:

Prayer Ventures
17437 Evener Way
Eden Prairie, Minnesota 55346
Phone: (612) 974-9240

This book is ideal for a six-week small group study. It can be used in adult education classes, midweek fellowship groups, home Bible studies, or prayer groups. To order this book or the other resources listed below, contact Prayer Ventures.

Books from Prayer Ventures:

Prayer Is a Welcome Place	$10.00
The Healing Moment—guide for healing prayer	$12.00
Miracle in the Making—great gift for new parents	$8.00

Audio Tapes from Prayer Ventures:

Healing Moments—devotional tool for relaxation and deepening your prayer life	$10.00
No More Walls—the power of prayer to break down barriers in relationships (3 cassettes)	$12.00
In the Shepherd's Care—inspiring story of six women who prayed for a friend with cancer	$5.00
The Gift of Hope and Healing—how to receive the gift of hope and healing, then give it to others	$5.00

Add $1.50 for shipping and handling per item. Please make checks and send orders to Prayer Ventures, 17437 Evener Way, Eden Prairie, Minnesota 55346.